LAND OF THE ROCK

OF THE ROCK

TALAMH AN CARRAIG

Heather Nolan

BREAKWATER

P.O. Box 2188, St. John's, NL, Canada, A1C 6E6

WWW.BREAKWATERBOOKS.COM

LIBRARY AND ARCHIVES CANADA CATALOGUING IN PUBLICATION
Title: Land of the Rock = Talamh an Carraig / Heather Nolan.
Other titles: Talamh an carraig
Names: Nolan, Heather, 1992- author.
Description: Poems.
Identifiers: Canadiana 20210374578 | ISBN 9781550819250 (softcover)
Classification: LCC PS8627.O586 L36 2022 | DDC C811/.6—dc23

We acknowledge the support of the Canada Council for the Arts, which last year
invested $153 million to bring the arts to Canadians throughout the country.
We acknowledge the financial support of the Government of Canada and
the Government of Newfoundland and Labrador through the Department of
Business, Tourism, Culture and Rural Development for our publishing activities.

Canada Council   Conseil des Arts
for the Arts   du Canada

Canadä

Newfoundland
Labrador

Breakwater Books is committed to choosing papers and materials for our books
that help to protect our environment.

This book is for Larry, for my sisters, for the family, and for everyone who has ever ventured into the unending questions of *who am I, and where do I come from?*

contents

part one

newfoundland

book one

southern shore

"I keep warm burning
bits of a house
the work of people who tried to live here."

John Steffler, *The Grey Islands*

mobile bay

my father denies
any connection to the place
his father was born,
or at least any attachment.

it's the people that matter, he says,
blowing on the rim of his teacup
what does a place mean
when they're gone?

then leaning in to my questioning,
he shows me the bruised sideboard,
knotted pine, pulled from the old house
he tore down with his own hands.

i see myself lean in to inspect heavy brass knobs
in the wavy mirror above, or at least
a shadow near enough to where i stand.
the two of us look like ghosts, unsolid.

returning to himself, he says *should've*
just burned the damn thing down,
but later digs out the land grant, sends an article
on the migration:

thousands of boats pouring west
from waterford, catching
on the southern shore like fish
in a net. *talamh an éisc.*

some of them didn't leave
and here we are like cracked foundations
and here we are and
here we are.

nolan's meadow

southern shore highway, drizzle
in patches. long scraggle of road
before mobile.

the meadow is falling down a cliff
pocked with sandstone piles,
lower part soggy with peat.

my ankles wet, i scare an old man
picking cranberries. *not a person alive
seen those houses*, he says,

tossing a gesture
to the steep slope above
where i find foundations, just piles of rock.

i dig, dank air reluctant
to participate, for some relic
to connect this place to you.

the east coast trail put up
a sign, nolan's meadow, but from
up here it's just a bare patch

of bluff. i imagine some hiker,
your teapot on their windowsill.
all i find are shards of purple glass,

blueberry bushes burnt with the coming
winter. piles of slate cleave beneath my boots
in satisfying ways.

intersection

i stop in witless bay for a cup of tea,
a place to get in out of the wind:
the irish loop coffee house. like everything here,
it stands on the edge.

proximity to the city evident
in the menu (avocado toast,
vegan tacos)—rurality
in the cooks coming out to chat.

i order the fishcakes,
try to stop the scale
from tipping me over the hill
and back into st. john's,

but to this crowd i will always be
a stranger. some hiker.

southern shore forest

patches of sun like pools
of gold, dazzling.

moss soft as a mother.
welcome home,
the kettle's on.

yet

the next step sinks, a wretched
squelch. shadows,
pots black as porter.

wooden boardwalk rotting back
into bog. behind me,
she says, *have you got a nickel*

for the fairies? and you stop
to admire their work.

mistaken point

we barely know each other and only meant
to drive to the trail in bay bulls, but impulsively
i say about the fossils at mistaken point.
and that first hundred kilometres, the thrill

of something new. stopping in ferryland to yell *fuck the
          british*
like it still matters, climb around an abandoned house
in aquaforte. daring him to tread swaying stairs, steal
          waxy lace curtains.
down the shore, i watch thin webs of houses around
          each little cove

grow farther apart. road a novelty in a land of the sea.
think of cousins in renews, catherine's stories of the
motley greying ornament clutched to an aunt's chest
          on the boat over.
the only part of us left made on irish soil.

by the time we reach the fields of rock at cappahayden,
we've run out of things to say. the barrens
impenetrable—late neoproterozoic miles open wide.
i feel myself pulled into the gaping past.

mistaken point. we don't even look for the fossils,
just stare silent out across the atlantic, a weather front
hanging low over churning waves. begin the long drive
            home,
watch the fog obliterate everything that lies behind.

abandoned house in aquaforte

sickly green of old man's beard
cascading from cupboard doors.
paint peels like lichen
on swollen chipboard.

we step high over settlements
of buckled floorboards, laid
by those who tried to root here. make it
to the kitchen. east corner wilted away

by time. in the empty space
where the wall once stood,
in and out of doors
exchange breath—

carpet thick with moss, kitchen sink tangled
in raspberry canes out front. no point
trying to keep anything out,
anything in.

field note

some surviving irish words in newfoundland english:[1]

scrob (from scríob) – "to scratch; to tear the flesh with claws or nails"

bresna (from brosna) – "a bundle of firewood; load of dry twigs"

dawnies (from donaidhe) – "miserable; in low health"

sleveen (from slíbhín) – "a sly deceitful man; a mean fellow; rascal; a mischievous child"

streel (from sraoille) – "a dirty, slovenly person, esp a woman"

angishore (from aindeiseoir) – "a weak, sickly person; an unlucky person deserving pity"

cosh (from cos) – "part of a river estuary cut off from the sea at low tide; place-name for such a lagoon"

---

[1] definitions are from the *Dictionary of Newfoundland English*.

feraun (from feorán curraigh) – "weed with yellow flowers and strong unpleasant odour; pineapple-weed"

lawnya vawnya (from lán an mhála) – "a good time at a dance or party; plenty to eat"

picnics with ancestors

when the grandkids are home,
my father arranges two cars, tupperware
crammed with sandwiches and sliced fruit.

my stepmom bakes scones,
asks my sister and me over her shoulder
on the trail to the nolan's meadow whether we feel
connected to this land our ancestors worked.

my sister shrugs, stops to check
on the children dodging alder brush.

i say it's more complicated than that.
dad in his unspoken way is looking out
for the old gate to the animal pasture.

stepping from cool spruce shade into the meadow,
we all hold our own disorientations. neglect
of generations grows dense as a thicket
and the meadow has retreated up the hill.

we try for a glimpse through the alder and stunted spruce.

then the children with the squeals of wet feet
and ant hills, and the lunch is hastily stowed
for another space quiet of our histories.

turning back i see my father lift a stone,
carry it to the rock piles farther down. first he is quiet,
but when he sees me watching, he says
"help the old fellas out. keep the stones from the field."

home and native

the nickname *the rock*
always called to mind some
jagged spire in hostile seas.
accurate enough,

with desperate people clinging
from cliffs, trying their damndest
to thrust down roots in a land
with no soil.

barren: where nothing can grow,
that wretched definition hovering
over people without a past, really,
because you aren't irish anymore

and don't you dare sing
"our home and
native land," you bastards,
reeking with the newness of settlers.

field note (conversations with my father)

q: how do you identify?

a: i identify as a newfoundlander
   more than anything. irish heritage,
   but newfoundlander.

q: what about canadian?

a: you got to remember,
   when i grew up there was still
   lots of people who didn't vote
   for confederation.

sirens i

"you aren't irish if you weren't born
on irish soil," aunt anne says, and i'm rigid,
not ready to concede.

what keeps coming back like a fox
to my garden is the question
of where. where am i from?

neat suburban houses in their vinyl suits
step back into the shadows of my mind,
as if to say, it's not me you're looking for.

the meadow presses against the back
of my head, warm
like an animal.

sirens call across the sea.
i call back. ask them to guide me.

they, of course, don't answer.

book two
tilting

"[I]n Newfoundland, the physical landscape has always been a striking feature of the place, and is noted as a contributing factor in the nature of the economy, settlement patterns, even the temperament of the people."

Vicki S. Hallett, "Continuous Erosion: Place and Identity in the Lives of Newfoundland Women"

fogo island ferry

moonrise fabric
slippery deck—
nothing smelled like fish.[2]
fogo.   return in all
seasons, never a breath warmer.
forgot the cooler, worry
what you're going to eat
a vegetarian on an
island island island.

covet small white structures in
vast spaces.   ceremonious blather
of rolling ferry rides
to islands removed from other
islands.   push yourself farther
remote. stand on the edge
of a cliff and dare
the isolation to advance.
fáilte go tilting. na mara.
wave wave wave.

---

[2] "nothing smelled like fish" spoken by Zita Cobb in Ted[x]Fort Townsend
event, March 11, 2012 (4:34): https://youtu.be/1dVDpvVwGWw.

arriving

driving into tilting, the first thing i see is irish flags,
rampaging in the wind, from every stick high enough
to hoist one. not fleming's pink, white and green the
townies love, either. orange. then i notice the signs all
in irish. fáilte go tilting.

houses painted white, proudly trimmed with a precious
bit of green. birch smoke pours from stovepipes. must
be twenty kilometres from the treed side of the island,
all barrens here.

it's below freezing now, though summer's barely over.
out here they talk about seven seasons, the way the ice
moves around them, but all i know is one. cold wind.

i stand there in the dark letting that sweet woodstove
musk wash over me and what i am thinking is—where
the hell did they get all this wood?

tilting, solid rock

lawn chairs on the deck
of the b & b, gouged wood
pummelled by salt.

wilderness rushing right up
to your doorstep: here
outdoors isn't a continuation
of place.

there is inside, shelter, and then
sea, where people go to work.
land

is less trustworthy—flat
and unyielding, solid
rock.

salt fish

for roy and christine dwyer

someone pops by to see if the innkeeper
wants any fish. perks up
when he sees me reading al pittman.
trust enters his eyes, tells me he's a writer.

sits for a coffee, shakes his head at
those architecture students, built some platform
on greene's point. *old fellas with handsaws could do
better. you have to think of what this place*

*was made of. what they had. what they made
with what they had.*

later, on the other side of the harbour,
i see him wave, shout from the top of his
driveway. i shout back. the wind carries this entire
exchange off without a word. when i reach the house

he says, *would you like to see some salt fish?*
in the shed are crates of onions, potatoes, cod,
opened bodies stiff as boards, spread on plastic
webbing. *used to use wood*, he says.

i wonder where he managed to find enough soil
to plant all these vegetables.

shows me the garden then, hauling up
beets like bricks as he talks—
glacial deposit, see? narrow strip of soil here.
straightens then, gets a good look at me.

where you from, then? town. not town.
stopping. starting. his wife, *come in*
for a coffee. slab of raisin cake. set of the
wrinkles around her eyes amused, like she's seen it all.

photos of the place when they used wood,
not plastic:

scattered houses. scattered fishermen. *no women*
allowed in those days, see. bad luck. photos of
the neighbours' daughter working an inshore boat.
trying to hide the pride, bursting with it.

i ask about the platform the mcgill kids did.
what's the good for it? stories happen in a
circle. not wide enough to make a circle on that.
raw spruce slashed by harsh angles and paint

honest red of stages below.

notes on lichen

landscapes of solid rock
and no rock in sight—

settled by blooms
putrid blue, yellow, white.
sickly reds. practically neon

in all this grey. rock's administration
fragile, encroached
upon. i'm overwhelmed by
respect for the audacity,

for an entity thriving
between grains of solid rock, vibrant
settlements crowned with sustainability.

fogo island inn

in foley's shed stories line the walls:
faded photographs pinned to clippings of the
       moratorium.
lines, hooks, sinewy snowshoes. garish glow
of the window shamrock casting green shadows
like bruises.

fáilte, the old clover says, *come on in*. and they come,
the tourists, long white suvs descending
from the inn. that sharp hulk towering stark
above the island, angles snagging on flinty coast.
the only straight lines in this place.

they always sit along one wall, watching, as though
this shed was a stage—and if offered a beer,
they want the blue bottled iceberg water.
something ancient distilled. they clap along
while the inn workers give the look, the *let's*
pick it up a notch, the *our guests pay*
to interact with authentic culture look.

later these folks with their blue bottles
and golf jackets will buy souvenir sou'westers, tell
anyone who'll listen how they kissed
a dead gaping fish. one of us now.

field note

fathom (n): a unit of measurement equal
to six feet, primarily used
when referring to the depth
of water.

 (v): to understand a particular
problem or enigmatic person
after much thought.

oliver's cove

so a rock feels no pain
and an island
never cries: a sentiment

empty until i climb the head
the day
the wind shut the ferry down.

like i've never seen the ocean before.
like i've never
seen a wave. massive swells assault

rock. white with rage or
is it play?
rote[3] like an elevator crashing.

air so cold it plunges into my guts
while
pockmarked tiny islands butt heads

with horizon, sea. but what makes an island
of a rock
that breaks the water's surface?

---

[3] "rote" refers to the sound of the sea in a particular cove.

indoors

wind crashes
over the house
in waves

we boil the kettle
here
this island.

gold

the morning so grey it's nearly purple.
through salt-crusted windows,

ribbons of gold cut the heft of cloud
above the harbour.

like fabric torn to
shreds

like a hair ribbon tangled
in branches

like tilting harbour saying,
hang on now.

there is harshness, yes,
but there is also this.

book three

sweet
bay

"There is nothing to learn from this
that we don't already know,
though we hope for revelations"

Agnes Walsh, "Southern Harbour, Two Cemeteries,
One Name"

day 0 – 8:30 pm

the night before the fall fishery opens,
people huddle along the shore
stare longingly at the water
nod, say, *rough weather tomorrow*.

a hunger in their eyes:
the food fishery only ten days,
and one of them gone
before it starts.

they meet in sheds, talk
of jobs and concerts in town,
drain bottles of beer
one eye always on the bay.

they speak
of meteorologists like gods,
forecasts like
promises.

---

[4] For ten days in late September, residents of Newfoundland are permitted to fish for cod. For many residents, this is a vital part of their diet for the winter, and their way of life. Late September in Newfoundland is hurricane season. "Recreational fishers are limited to five groundfish per day (including cod)" ("2018 Newfoundland and Labrador recreational groundfish fishery," Department of Fisheries and Oceans website, https://www. dfo-mpo.gc.ca/fisheries-peches/decisions/fm-2018-gp/atl-18-eng.html).

day 0 – 10:00 pm

field note

the institution of "the shed" in rural newfoundland
takes the place of the pub. a place to gather.

day 1 – 5:30 am

at dawn, a few hands head to the wharf
for a look, but they know.
land makes the real laws
out here. cursing the calm waters yesterday,
perfect weather. should've gone anyways.

and why not?

what good is bureaucracy with a storm
coming in, and only ten days
to stock the freezers
for winter?

the only sound: waves
slapping the wharf. black water
thick as oil. the gulls look away.

day 1 – 2:00 pm

i

all day the wind pushes
harder. the whole cove
turned inward—smoke
darting quick from stovepipes away.

i totter along the shore,
soggy. people call out to see
if i need a lift someplace—i shake
my head.

my face grows rough,
hard as limestone,
patterns carved where the rain
cuts in.

the horizon line billows
like silk.

ii

and all day the wind
gets meaner. in kitchen windows
murmurs start
about if it doesn't let up

by tomorrow. later we'll gather,
fill glasses, try to forget
the day gone. the sly
streaks of silver,

glinting past in the night.

day 2 – 11:00 am

the notion of trees as sturdy
disappears quickly, whole trunks
bending down to touch
the ground. bouncing back
the other way, spring-loaded.

the aspen out front winks
and then turns a backflip.

day 3 – 9:00 am

bill hoses gull shit off the splitting table,
hauls up gaping, pucker-lipped cod.
shaking his head—four or five at best.
feels for gills with numb sausage fingers,
turns them to fillets with two quick swings
of the knife. tosses the heads
to gulls weeping hungry
like children.

the rest he leaves whole
for his mother. *the old folks*, he says,
don't waste a thing. stew it all.

the next crew stumbles onto the wharf,
loads out empty buckets.
saying *well, we made it back ourselves.*

day 3 – 11:00 am

roddy in the window with binoculars, tracing
every boat that does venture out.
*they're drifting, see? won't catch anything
like that.* coat and boots on,

ready to take off if the wind
changes. sat there since six running
commentary, checking charts.
*nobody's caught a thing. arse is supposed
to drop out of 'er around noon.*

the wind was supposed to be gone. he swears.
they said it was going to be gone.

day 4 – 6:00 pm

for mary maloney

i overhear mary say *i'm just creative enough*
to be dangerous, and i am drawn

like a codfish to a hooked squid:
senseless, mouth open, baited.

her piercing blue eyes, laugh lines
puckish, proud simper drawn to grin

i think, here's a hard ticket.
i think, here's my kind of woman.

she talks of her poetry with the hushed pride
of dissension. *when the fish plant closed down,*

someone had to do it. she sits back,
sips her whiskey.

i dream of mary, the next poet laureate,
and how it ought not be any other way.

day 5 – 2:00 am

deep dark, walking home along the shore road.
waving off the fuss of flashlights. spinning,
face up, gulping the giddy mass
of stars. great bowl of them coming down
over me. flicking my head this way and that,
trying to catch their winking! going dizzy
with the obliqueness of trying not to look
them in the eye.

dizzy,

then—christ! dawn barely hours away.
let the whiskey haul me up the bank.
get some sleep. try again.

day 5 – 10:00 am

not a clock in this house
seems to have the right time,
some hours off.

i like this. time
just another senseless regulation
imposed by the dfo.[5]

days measured by weather—
when the rain stops.
when the wind drops out.

by the destruction of hurricanes—
it was like this since igor.
like that before gabriel.

[5] Department of Fisheries and Oceans

day 6

wind.

day 7 – 4:00 pm

the mayor just some guy with a summer house up the
road. first thing he did was bring up putting a coffee
shop on the wharf. everyone uneasy then, couldn't
fathom what you'd want with coffee down on the
wharf. idleness a bother in their workspace. he said
about the tourism and they just stared so he left it at
that. he went and got a grant then to put a hiking trail
in, got to hire on a summer student and everything.
but the thing washed away with the first big wind.
now he just drives along the main road, listens to folks
complain about the quotas. nods his head. goes on to
the next house.

day 8 – 1:00 pm

sea glass like ghosts
of resettlement, still
drifting in from the islands.

shores deemed too remote,
not making the cut
for canada. unmoored

in a brackish place
between colony and
confederation, smooth stones

tumble on, make it to shore.
smoothed by the journey,
no edges left to fit back together.

stories and bottles forgotten,
glued to form sailboats, anchors, icons
in craft stores up the cape.

day 9 – 9:30 am

the only difference
between
      sea glass
       and
           garbage

is a jagged edge.

day 10 – 8:00 pm

the difficulty of translation
within the same language—
is it colloquialism or circumstance,

the way a newfoundlander says
yes, *yup*, on the sharp
intake of breath—
nearly a gasp,
preparing for the sigh that follows,
                                  measured by

the weight of air, rather than compliance:
a melancholy exchange
of breath and sound,
communication of a specific
                        harshness

like wind that slices the skin.

like an empty net emerging
from the god damned water.

part two

ireland

book four

waterford

"We come

to kneel at the doorway,
to peer into that kind of

dark. To think our way
backwards, listening."

Kelly Norah Drukker, "At the Seven Churches
(Na Seacht dTeampaill)"

further

dear grandmother—though it's further than that—
i came to tell you of a place
(did no one report back?)
of talamh an éisc, to smell
the dirt of your boggy
black earth, search through names
on cracked celtic crosses
desperate for some substance of belonging.

grandmother—well, further than that—
what made you stay
on this sodden island
while your sons boarded ships?
and what do you make
of the irony, your kin
barrelled
by the same north atlantic wind they fled?

salting codfish for winter when they traded
waterford for mobile: do you think
they felt cheated?
some noxious undertaking
that tumbled them west past cork—no, further—

crossing that wretched ocean
only to find themselves on another
isle of rock, stunned by the same colonial power.

or anyway, grandmother—further, yes—
what do you make of this plot and
what makes a body irish? i know
it's been a while but do you think
i could squeeze another stone
next to yours? temple bar has made me woozy
and they're just playing
the same old songs from home.

mount misery

strange to be cast so far inland. a river city. the suir splits
waterford from kilkenny's banks, where on the cliff above
perches a painted rock in blue or orange, depending on
who's winning. nobody will say what the prize might be. i try
to imagine relations long dead, leaving rotting crops to trace
the line of this river to a ship that would toss them to open
waters. learning to walk with sea legs that would come natu-
rally further down the line. a desperation in leaving solid
ground, in trading irishness—for what? for generations
peering back while accents slowly fade?

here there is no coastal breeze, just air dense as murky
water.
lungs stretch wide as though casting out of my body in
search of salt air.

the sea beckons me homeward.

in waterford
listening

first the murky blossom, then
the pint settles black. listening,

with fingertips to dewy glass, for something
i can recognize, some linguistic lineage not forgotten.

and like a radio dial finding its place, the connection
comes and sizzles. i hear it! *how ya getting*

on. yes b'y. the hard a. the soft t. voices drifting
from the back of the pub and i'm drawn in.

first by the outward humour of people used
to entertaining, but when it settles, i see

it covers something darker. older. an estranged
sibling of the same childhood trauma, i listen

for what speech patterns can tell us, how
these islands share a history of malnutrition.

field note

shared colloquialisms between newfoundland and
waterford, as overheard in pubs:

townie: someone from the city

waddayat?: what's up?

wha: a light, wispy sound, meaning "what?" in a "could
you repeat what you just said" sort of way

how ya gettin' on?: how are you?

what are you saying?: what's up?

deadly: good

yes b'y: general noise of assent or surprise

to go on a tear: to go on a bout of drinking/partying

is as talamh an éisc mé

when i think *i'm after hearing this before*,
i don't realize the connection
of that linguistic phenomenon[6]—

grandfather's language bulky
and heavy on my tongue. my sister says
why the hell would you learn

a dead language?[7] but i press on
long enough to learn to say
is as talamh an éisc mé,[8]

ignore the suggestion
that it would be easier
to just say ceanada.

---

[6]   The linguistic phenomenon would be the after-perfect, a tense that exists in
      Newfoundland English as a direct translation from Irish.

[7]   Irish Gaelic is not a dead language. My sister is dumb.

[8]   *Is as talamh an éisc mé*—i am from newfoundland.

ní ceanadaigh sinn[9]

ag stad bus éireann i bport láirge,
cheistigh an fear:
cad as tú? agus deirim:

is ó thalamh an éisc mé,
cá bhfuil sé sin? a fhiafraíonn sé
féachaim ar an fharraige, saoirse.

deirim: tá sé i gceanada

---

[9] we are not Canada

at a bus érieann stop in waterford
the man speaks:
where are you from, yourself? and i say

i am from newfoundland.
him: *where is that?* i look
at the sea, the freedom.

i say, it's in canada.

book five

the
burren

marsh greens
disappear abruptly

when the bus climbs into the hills
of the burren.

massive mounds of shredded limestone
we circle toward

from a distance
a wasteland
of solid rock, waiting

to show you the difference.

some field notes on the burren from afar

bedrock pools like liquid on the hill,
like lava, still cooling, holding heat.
i trail my fingers over limestone's grit,
feel the grooves where raindrops dig in deep.

they say the change the landscape made was quick.
one generation to the next, the earth
was overgrazed by cattle herds and sheep,
eroding soil down to what was left:

a karstic field of rock where nothing grows,
or so you'd think to see it from afar.
this rock, a consequence of what was lost,
and yet as i get closer i can see

that every crack and every gryke is filled
with soil where lime itself leached deep.
in every space, mosses running wild
and even orchids climb between the rocks.

when sunlight crowns, a golden light winks
on the softness of limestone's ragged face.

field note

landscape is the visual backdrop of a place.
place is visceral: the land we reckon with.

night on the burren

the way the dusk gathers,
a week before the solstice—long
and lean, a moony blue dripping
from limestone.

we trace circles up the hill
in echoing air, close yet
wide open
to the table tomb, poll na mbrón

older than the pyramids, he says,
shaking his head.
the past here
unfathomable.

nearly midnight, dark falls
like a gavel. he's still pointing out landmarks,
through windows thick as turf now.
deep black. headlights just enough

to show we're still here.

sirens ii

the next day i try to remember
his directions—the tossed hand
in the night, rural village black
see the church up ahead?

but i didn't (no light) and i try
to recall. right at the church.
on past the graveyard. sun blazing,
beads forming under the one rumpled blouse

from my suitcase as i climb
the hill, surveying stones.
he loves me. he loves me not.
at the studio, prodding woollen spools, waiting

for the tourists to leave. him out,
deliveries to ballyvaughan.
the worker uncomfortable. *shall
i tell him you called?* shows me his hands,

covered in oil—
and i remember. his plan to rebuild
an ancient knitting machine, stitching
tradition to technology, the conversation

blossoming fresh from the pub last night. ways
to bring the past forward. i tug at the fancy blouse,
burning to leave before he returns.
wipe away the mascara. get back to work.

field note

is carraig mé.
is oileán mé.

grotto

weeks searching
fields of barren rock,
and i see it:

lilting granite mary,
her unmistakeable form
jutting above the stone fields
of fanore.

i imagine villagers clutching
rosaries, breath short,
pushing back the boundary
as they hike from green fields below.

this, a place. golden glow of it
shrouding the old statue.
and around it, open hills of landscape,
where a rock is just a rock.

pastoral

this was the way i showed up:
suitcase clatter, hair like a gale,
bent on some drafty cottage gloom
smell of torched turf lure

but i couldn't afford that notion, settled
for electric kettles in bright hostel kitchens
staring at maps, places i'd rather be. ideally,
a rental car, long ambling drives.
really, cross-referenced bus tables, google searches. all
            that wifi.

taking walks into town, aware
of vibrant painted tourist shops;
knowledge that meant i wasn't
a tourist. this was the way i showed up.

but this landscape reveals itself slowly, like strata,
and the slate-grey lake i sought floods in
when the first drops fall from darkened skies and
definitions dissolve like chalk on the surface.

like the bedrock, i feel exposed.

when the time comes

rock walls line the fields
flashing past the bus windows
a patchwork.

stones not mortared
or laid like bricks,
rather fit together, ready
to move on when the time comes
should it come.

i start to write a letter
then
tear out the page.

two ways

i

on the horizon, glinting
the aran islands
soft as sirens
beckoning

ii

the aran islands ahead like a dream
like moons
erratics tossed from clare's shores
by angry glaciers
old giants.

book six

inis oírr

"Without other accompanying measures,
reinventing rurality as a tourist commodity
is a band-aid on the gaping wounds of history."

Ursula A. Kelly, "Learning from Loss: Migration,
Mourning and Identity"

late for the ferry
to inis oírr

the only seats left on the top deck.
tourists braced, swathed in bright gore-tex.
sky dark as a dream.

the owner of the b & b back in doolin warned
of a storm coming in, heady winds in galway bay.
a wildness in some of the faces around me,
the mad desire to feel the sea,

grinning teeth flecked with salt.
and i feel it too. mad for the naval burst
of a cresting wave. mad
for the feel of the sea like a lover.

when the ferry gets in

island folks line up along the dock
offering tours in the family car
faces eroded by the rain.

horses tethered to carriages scuff their feet.
every hour another eruption
of colourful rain jackets
spills from the pier,

climbs the hill to the old castle
chatter ringing like church bells
into quiet air, blowing
like gulls away on the next boat.

not many tourists
when it rains,

says the shopkeeper, as i dig out 50 cents
for the postcard, casting wildly around
for something else to add to the total.

damp ebbs and flows through
gaps in the windows, doors,
the chill itself browsing wool sweaters.
walls defenceless against the atlantic.

and by god, a place like this
surviving on the tourist money,
depending on the weather.
the shopkeeper nods. knows.

teashop on inis óirr

old gaelic melody in a woozy lull from the radio
mixes with damp when the door blows open. i warm my
        hands
over soup-bowl steam, flex and stretch stiff knuckles.
at the next table, folks from other islands

compare notes on the tourism trade and being
        surrounded by ocean
how isle of wight has gotten pretty posh these days,
all those dfls—down from london—buying holiday
        homes
good for the economy, sure, but something is being
        erased.

the server looks through foggy windows toward
        overgrown fields,
wild rose and mallow run like streels though pastures
        long forgotten
by those who've gone somewhere, looking for
        something.
the english ask about the old castle crumbling on the hill.

she laughs. *there was nothing special about it, just some rich family from clare, built it and were gone again.*

edges i

on the edge of an island, that's
where you corner yourself. that last spit
of rock you've never gone past,
held back by immeasurable

force—leave the island the dignity
of slipping soundlessly back to water.
all around, waves push
from other places. knock

against the edges that
surround you, gathered into
the ragged cloth of coastline.

husky mounds of the maumturks

shadowy with the storm, rising
stark from the sea between me and connemara.

remembering stumbling back
from the pub through tunnels
of rock wall.

was it the guinness or
the velvety dark
that chose the wrong

path? and which of the
squat beige houses
was the b & b?

behind me, a neat stack
of euros sat coy
on the bar,

attention drawn
to ignorance of custom.
where you from then.

where where where.
where. are. you.
from.

and now as i watch the clouds congeal,
i notice the coins still there,
tipping not the thing here.

some tourist.

last ferry

cold now, the damp starting to matter.
wind on wet clothes, pressing
in. and the waves again, pointing back
toward doolin. the storm nipping at our heels,
the last boat across today.

swells climb over the top deck,
windows turn to walls
of grey and we rise,
crashing down,
carrying on.

tourists clutching walls, stumbling
into each other. heaving into bags.
the locals darting around
handing out paper towel.
captain serene at the window,
watching the view.

turning back i see the island lean
over the channel
to whisper with inis meáin.

edges iii

i

erosion shows
which way water chose
to cut
desperate for departure

scars of going
ruts worn in
by all those
who have left before you

water slowly, slowly washes
the face of rock
just as your own identity
erodes, leaving your skin

soft and blank as a baby,
your spine curved
at the shoulder, in the city
you say has swallowed you whole

ii

gravity defies the marrow
of your pelvic bone, sloshing
like the swells
on which you leave this island.

acknowledgements

Writing this book was only possible through the contributions of many generous people sharing their stories and conversations, and for that I am deeply grateful.

Thanks to Roy Dwyer, Christine Dwyer, Al Dwyer, Tom Earle and Tilting Harbour B&B, Paddy Barry, Maureen Foley, Phil Foley, Dan Greene, Larry Nolan, Mary Byrne, Alex Stead (for putting up with my miserably slow hiking while I jotted notes about fairies), Catherine Ikin, Joe Brazil, Mary Maloney, Bill Maloney, Rod Byrne, John Maloney, Patti Maloney, Tom Philpott, and everyone who conspired to help me get in a boat during the ridiculously windy food fisheries of 2018 and 2019.

Go raibh maith agaibh Dean, Aodhan, Alan, An Uisce Beatha (in nearly every sense of the words), Doolin Dinghy Books, the lovely folks at Aras Ghleann Cholm Cille, Diarmuid, Mounir, Kerstin, Thomas, Joni, Ivan, Tiffany George, Sean Bradley, Rachel, Karen, Smiley, and the crew,

for the good craic and important lessons about getting a
lift, and all the wonderful folks I have met in Ireland these
last few years.

Thank you, Beth Follett, Matthew Hollett, and Joan
Sullivan, for writing recommendations for grant
applications. Your kind letters pushed me forward.
Thank you, ArtsNL and Canada Council for the Arts, for
granting that funding.

Thank you, Mary Dalton, Robert Finley, Andreae Callanan,
Karen Solie, the Memorial University creative writing
program, and especially the 3901 and 4913 creative writing
classes of 2018–19. Thank you, Adèle Barclay and *ARC
Magazine*. Your guidance, mentorship, and kindness have
made all the difference.

Thank you, Agnes Walsh and Claire Wilkshire for your
care and attention in editing this manuscript. Thank you,
Jocelyne Thomas, Rebecca Rose, and the whole team at
Breakwater Books.

Thank you to my wonderful agent, Stephanie Sinclair.

Thank you, Doug Walbourne-Gough, for your ever-
generous mentorship and friendship; Jane Walker, Allie
Duff, Andreae and Mark Callanan, Nate Little, Kelly
Drukker, the O'Reilly and Nolan clans, Matt Howse and
the late Broken Books, Russell Cochrane, Tommy Duggan,
and all the wonderful people who have inspired my
writing, whether they know so or not.

The Irish Studies and Centre for Newfoundland Studies collections at the QE2 Library and the A. C. Hunter Library in St. John's were massively important resources in my research for this book. Public libraries are vital. Fund them.

Thank you, Larry Nolan, for always fact-checking my geology metaphors and sneaking food into my fridge.

Several poems in this collection first appeared in earlier forms in the *Antigonish Review*, *EVENT*, *Riddle Fence*, *Janus Unbound*, *nqonline*, *Viator*, and *Nine Muses Poetry*. "Home and Native Land" was on the CBC Poetry Prize Longlist in 2017. A selection from the Tilting portion of this collection was also read at Memorial University of Newfoundland's English Undergraduate Conference in 2018. Thank you for giving my work a space.

Quotations at the beginning of each section come from the following works, which inspired this one in many ways: *The Grey Islands*, by John Steffler; the essay by Vicki S. Hallett "Continuous Erosion: Place and Identity in the Lives of Newfoundland Women"; and the essay by Ursula A. Kelly "Learning From Loss: Migration, Mourning and Identity," from the book *Despite This Loss: Essays on Culture, Memory and Identity in Newfoundland and Labrador*; *Oderin*, by Agnes Walsh; and *Small Fires*, by Kelly Norah Drukker.

Thank you, Graham xo

HEATHER NOLAN is a neurodiverse writer from St. John's, NL. She is the author of *This Is Agatha Falling* (Pedlar Press, 2019), which was longlisted for the BMO Winterset Award and the ReLit Award. She has published poetry and prose across Canada, the US, and the UK. She was the winner of the Gregory J. Power Poetry Award, and was longlisted for the CBC Poetry Prize. This is her first poetry collection.